She Who Waits

How to Patiently Wait on God for Your Mate

Alfreda Jones

She Who Waits. Copyright © 2012 by Alfreda Jones Ministries.
All rights reserved.

No part of this publication may be reproduced or transmitted in any form or by any means, electronic or mechanical, including photocopy, recording, or any information storage and retrieval systems, without written permission from the publisher, except in the case of brief quotations embodied in critical articles and reviews.

Printed in the United States of America.

ISBN-10: 0615623492
ISBN-13: 978-0615623498

Published & Distributed By:
Alfreda Jones Ministries

www.shewhowaits.org

Print Formatting: NyShell Imari Unlimited
www.nyshellimari.com

DEDICATION

This book is dedicated to my wonderful children Joshua, Asia, Dana, my beautiful granddaughter Miyanna, and my parents Audrey Jones and the late Cleveland Jones, Sr.

My father taught me from a very young age that I am a precious jewel and should be treated as such. Allow God the father to teach you how valuable you are in His sight.

Do you feel like you're constantly choosing "Mr. Wrong"?

Do you believe your mate has already been pre-determined by God?

In past relationships do you ask yourself "What Was I Thinking?"

CONTENTS

Acknowledgements — i
Introduction — 1
Behold — 3

PART 1
1 She Who Waits on the Lord — 5
2 The Desire's of a Woman's Heart — 7
3 Common Challenges — 9

PART 2
4 Getting to Know God the Father — 17
5 Your Will vs. God's Will — 25
6 Setting Standards — 27

PART 3
7 'Mr. Right" or "Mr. What was I Thinking?" — 31
8 Mr. Right Questionnaire — 37

PART 4
9 Preparing for Your Mate Questionnaire — 43
10 Defining a Virtuous Woman — 47

PART 5
11 A Letter to Our Daughters — 59
Author's Final Thoughts — 61

ACKNOWLEDGEMENTS

Special thanks to my friends, family, pastors and everyone who helped with the development of this book. Most of all, thanks to All Mighty God! You are my EVERYTHING!

INTRODUCTION

The purpose of this book is to help you gain spiritual insight into relationships, dating, and how to patiently wait for your mate.

John 8:32 says, "And you shall know the truth, and the truth shall make you free". It is one thing to know the truth but the truth will not make you free unless you actually do something with it. This scripture coincides with James 1:22, "But be doers of the word, and not hearers only, deceiving yourselves." I want to elaborate on the "do". I want to discuss the things that will help you walk through the process of God's will as it relates to dating and relationships. We are taught the word of God and often times we get the legalistic perspective: the do's and don'ts. However, the truth is, we are human, in physical bodies and we have emotions. I want to give you information that will help you in this journey.

To make things perfectly clear, I am not saying I have never done anything wrong. I am coming from a position of transparency. I will share my experiences and what it means to wait on God for your mate. I understand that sometimes the goal seems unreachable, but it is attainable. You will know you are not alone in this journey.

I hope that some part of this book will benefit you. Use what you can, share with those who need direction and encouragement and most of all, let it be a reminder that God is for you and you can trust Him.

BEHOLD

SHE ARRIVES

She sits, She gleams,

Behold her, in all her beauty

Behold her, in her truth.

Yes, she is lovely, yes, she is refined, no, there is but one like her

Behold,

A Queen

SHE EXPOUNDS

As she speaks, she chimes - her tone both inviting and warm.

Each word,

Shadowed by wisdom and presented upon a royal plate of grace.

In her speech, gentle whispers, whispers, whispers –

Echoing God's voice

SHE STANDS

Head high, shoulders back, eyes direct, her walk commands alone.

She sees clearly, she is wise.

Do you not know whom you are beholding?

Has she been taught?

Does this come naturally?

Is such refinement necessary?

Alfreda Jones

The answer lies in the question.
You ask if she has been taught, as you deem her proficient.
You ask if it comes naturally, as you mirror her gestures.
You ask if such refinement is necessary,
Yet it holds you speechless.

Her preparation has been her time with The King.
It is His love that nurtures her.
It is His hand that molds her.
It is His patience, His gentleness, His ever increasing voice that
Governs her

Her head is high because He raised it.
Her speech is poised because He speaks through her.
Her love is powerful, even to the piercing of hearts because it
belongs to Him; it is the love of The King that is her weapon.

Who she was is in the past.
Who she is draws your attention.
Who she will soon become is yet to astonish.

He unapologetically presents her as His beloved.

Behold,

A Queen

SHE WHO WAITS ON THE LORD

If you research the history of queens, princesses, or royal and mighty women of God, you will see common threads. These women walk different, their speech is articulate, and their confidence level generally exceeds that of other women. When a woman knows her value she is intrinsically powerful and it exudes in her personality.

As a woman you were destined to be a queen from the day you were born. Even in your mother's womb. You may believe you were born for one of the following reasons:

- To marry and be a helpmate to your husband
- To work, worship and be a witness for Christ

Technically, both answers are correct so you do not have to choose. However, there is a divine order. Foremost, we are placed on earth to worship God, be a witness for Christ and for the work of the ministry. While it may be in God's will for us to marry, the bible says,

> Seek ye first the kingdom of God and his righteousness and all these things will be added unto you (Matthew 6:33).

Please note that this scripture says to seek God before seeking a mate. Although it sounds simple, this is one of the most challenging areas for single Christian women. It is God's will that you become married to the person He has destined and prepared for you, His precious daughter.

It will be in the time and season He has pre-determined for you. Although there are many seasons in the natural, there are spiritual seasons. I truly believe there are different times in your life you are ready to be married and if you are aligned spiritually and the man is aligned spiritually it would be considered God ordained BUT you may not be ready physically, mentally or emotionally. You should be complete. That does not mean you have to be perfect, but confident in these areas of your life.

Bottom line, if you are seeking to please God with your whole heart you are becoming spiritually aligned for the mate God has for you. The bible says,

> Take delight in the Lord, and he will give you
> the desires of your heart (Psalm 37:4).

There is not one specific person for you. You can be compatible and equally yoked with more than one man; you have a choice who you will marry. But in order for the match to be God-ordained, you must be equally yoked.

2
THE DESIRES OF A WOMAN'S HEART

Do not ever feel guilty for having the desire to marry. Women were created to be helpmates: the strong desire to be married is natural.

As women we must realize that because we are such emotional beings, we tend to make decisions from our emotions and not our spiritual intellect. This is why is it so important to ask God and seek godly counsel when making decisions that will impact our destiny and purpose.

The word of God says, "Keep your heart with all diligence, for out of it spring the issues of life" (Proverbs 4:23). It is so important to take heed to this biblical warning because at times the heart may not easily distinguish hurt, harm or deception. This can make us susceptible to abuse.

When waiting on God's ideal mate we sometimes become anxious. Instead of waiting patiently and graciously, we start the search ourselves rather than letting the man find us. The Bible tells us, "He who finds a wife finds a good thing, and obtains favor from the Lord" (Proverbs 18:22). When years exceed our timeframe for marriage this becomes a challenge. We tend to compromise, forget our queen status and make ourselves available to men who are not God's will for us.

Don't be discouraged. We've all walked down that path at some point in our lives.

3
COMMON CHALLENGES

You must remember that God knows who your mate is before he was created in his mother's womb. God is simply preparing your husband and it is not wise to receive him before God has released him to you. Realistically, we face challenges every day that can get us off track. While these challenges are common, they do not have to deter us from receiving what God has for us if we are aware of them.

FEAR

Sometimes the spirit of fear sneaks in and attacks your faith. When this happens, you may try to assist God in finding your mate by seeking a man yourself. You can make yourself available but you should not pursue the man. Yet, keep in mind he is not going to drop out of the sky. As women of God, we go to church or home and unless he goes to our church or lives near us, we may not meet anyone. We have to be open about attending events and socializing outside of our normal circle.

Seek God, the Holy Spirit, and godly counsel in this area. As a Godly woman you must be sure when your future husband presents himself to you. In other words, even after years of living for God, the enemy will try to attack by presenting someone who appears to be sent by God.

LONELINESS

Can I be transparent? I believe that because women have different characteristics and personalities, there is no <u>one</u> way to overcome the spirit of loneliness. To combat loneliness most of us call a best friend, immerse ourselves in work or when that fails, fall into depression. The enemy (Satan) knows the power of loneliness and he uses it to discourage us and attack our faith. At times the attack can be so strong that you may feel the mate God has created for you will never find you. That is not true!

TEMPTATION

I want to give attention to Godly dating. You need to remember that a godly man is still a man and you are still a woman. Do not be fooled - you can be tempted! Keep this in mind and be careful. Women are made for men and we are drawn to them – especially a strong, godly man.

Satan will always try to hinder God's plan for you. That is why it is so important to keep strong godly people in your life for accountability. If the enemy can knock you off track and get you to do things outside of God's will and timing, he can catapult you into the wilderness where you will spend precious time wandering aimlessly and your mate could be nearby. The closer you are to attaining your husband, the more the enemy is going to try every tactic to deter the union from occurring. For example have you ever heard of two people dating, aligning themselves up with the word of God and all of sudden interest begin to peak from everyone! This is a tactic.

Merriam-Webster Dictionary defines temptation as, "the act of tempting or the state of being tempted especially to evil: enticement". God knows that we are tempted by our nature but He also gives us the ability to not surrender to the temptation. The bible says, "No temptation has overtaken you except such as is common to man; but God is faithful, who will not allow you to be tempted beyond what you are able, but with the temptation will also make the way of escape, that you may be able to bear it " (I Corinthians 10:13).

To simplify, you never just "fall into sin". You have to make a conscious decision to sin. There is absolutely no benefit to risking the gifts and blessings God has for you. Is this a risk you are willing to take? If you are dealing with temptation, it is because the enemy wants to destroy you. With all that is within you resist. Build yourself up in faith, use wisdom and do not allow your walk to be compromised or hindered.

VULNERABILITY

Traumatic events, loss, feelings of inadequacy, rejection, and low self-esteem can all lead to vulnerability. When we are vulnerable, we may do things we normally would not do. This is not the time to make relationship decisions. To prevent yourself from falling into sin during these times, build yourself up in God through prayer, fasting and consecration. We usually succumb to our vulnerabilities when we have not been built up spiritually. That means we have a relationship issue with God (not a man). Keep in mind that where your mind is, your body follows.

Talk to someone you trust during these times. Believe it or not this can be a time of quiet desperation. We can become less transparent when we are vulnerable. We do not want anyone to know what we are going through. That is Satan's plan; keep it a secret and suffer in silence. However, it is not God's plan.

GUILT

If you are a single parent, guilt can become a large factor when considering a mate. "Is it okay to date?", or "Do I have to wait until my children are grown?" are common questions. Children are impressionable and mothers are often concerned about being role models. We believe our children view us as non-human; they don't see us as being emotional beings that have feelings and need love. When we begin dating, their perspective of us may change. Our children may not want the dynamics of the family to change, especially if you have been single for an extended period of time. Be encouraged and do not go it alone. If your children begin to shows signs that they have problems with you dating, address it.

THERE IS HOPE

As Godly women, we have met many of the quotas laid out for us; attend church, support ministry, fellowship with the saints, pay your tithes and so on. However, at the end of the day we all have various challenges but desire the same result, a Godly mate. Knowing the enemy's tactics, we are better prepared to fight. Although these weapons may be formed against you, they will not prosper if you stand on the word. Confessing God's word will strengthen you.

"As women we must realize that because we are such emotional beings, we tend to make decisions from our emotions and not our spiritual intellect."

4
GETTING TO KNOW GOD THE FATHER

Many of us are stuck in religion and do not understand citizenship in the Kingdom of God.

Kingdom living is having a real relationship with God. This relationship helps you understand God and His will for your life. Religion is about looking Godly but kingdom is about relationship with God. The point is this, kingdom living is how God operates, not religion. To attain what God has for you, you must live according to His word. Acknowledge, understand and believe what God has in store for you.

THE HOLY SPIRIT

The Holy Spirit is a gift from God. He speaks to our spirit, teaches us, comforts us and gives us direction. When the Holy Spirit leads us, we will be able to discern right from wrong. We must be in tune with and led by the Holy Spirit. Otherwise we will make decisions before we seek God and then have the audacity to ask Him to bless our choices! When we are spiritually in tune, we are able to discern the spirit a person is carrying and if it is of God.

The Holy Spirit wants you to fall in love with Him first! Many women make the mistake of falling in love with a man and then make excuses for not being able to fellowship with others. They tend to put their all into the man and the relationship while putting the things of God second. God is jealous. He wants your heart first. If you give your heart to the Almighty God, then and only then will He give you the desires of your heart.

PRAYER

The more we commune with God, the more we are able to discern his voice. When we spend time in prayer, we will become more acquainted with Him. Becoming acquainted means building a relationship.

FASTING

Biblical fasting is abstaining from food for a spiritual purpose. It draws you into a deeper, more intimate and powerful relationship with the Lord. God shows us that spending time with Him through fasting empowers us over our fleshly desires. As a woman of God, your main focus should be pleasing God. Fasting is a weapon and a strategy that will draw you closer to God and sharpen your discernment. Fasting may also help you know if it is Mr. Right or Mr. Wrong approaching you.

GODLY COUNSEL

Although God speaks to us directly, there are times when He will speak to Godly men and women in your life about you, particularly your pastors. So, do not always think that He is going to come to you and reveal things through a vision or a dream.

SEEK GOD'S FACE

Speaking from personal experience, there is nothing more powerful and anointed than seeking God's face for strength and direction. When you feel alone and no one understands what you are going through, you can implement some of the following ways to enter the presence of God:

1. Begin to Pray – Find a quiet, private place in your home where you can pray without interruption.

2. Pray in the Spirit – Praying in tongues takes you into a deeper, more intimate realm with God.

3. Worship – When you begin to worship God, you usher in His presence. Playing your favorite worship CD can help

usher in the Holy Spirit. To usher in the spirit means to invite God (the Holy Spirit) into your heart; an open invitation to welcome His Presence.

4. Spiritual Bath – Taking a spiritual bath is powerful and anointed. I use the fragrances Myrrh and Frankincense. These fragrances are used for bodily cleansing. While using them, ask God to cleanse your mind, soul and body.

5. Journaling – As you begin to seek God more, He will begin to reveal things to you in ways you have never experienced. He may wake you in the middle of the night, prompting you to pray or He may reveal something to you in a vision or a dream. Keep a journal next to your bed so you can write down any revelation He gives you. If you do not write them down, you may not fully remember what God was saying.

It is beneficial to journal on a daily basis in addition to writing what God reveals to you. Hopefully, as a result of journaling you will see patterns, particularly as you build your relationship with God. Journaling documents your frame of mind, it will give you a perspective of your mental and emotional capacity. It is especially beneficial to journal if you are involved in a relationship. Journaling during relationships helps you keep track of your thinking in that season of your life.

"The more we commune with God, the more we are able to discern his voice."

5
YOUR WILL vs. GOD'S WILL

God works in divine order. When we operate outside of His principles and divine order, and on our own accord, it leads to struggle and failure. When we choose God's will, it leads to life and success. He is our creator and knows the best direction for us. When we are not living in our created purpose, we fall into the vicious cycle of allowing our flesh to determine our choices.

If we permit the world's wisdom to define us, we will measure our success according to the world's standards and allow the world to make choices for us. Because we do not know everything God has in store for us, many of us go through life playing Russian roulette, taking chances, picking our own mate without consulting God. As a result, we end up in relationships that rob us of our emotional fortitude.

Until God sends your mate, walk in your queenly anointing. Remember, you do not want to waste any time on someone that is not God's choice for you. So trust God with your whole heart and he will direct you.

6
SETTING STANDARDS

As a queen and a beautiful woman of God, you need to set standards in every area of your life, especially in dating and relationships. The problem is, before you can set any standards, you have to know who you are, whose you are (God's) and God's purpose for your life.

From a natural perspective, women are emotional beings with a strong desire to please others. From the day we were created, we have often made the error of making decisions from our emotions and flesh and not being led by the Holy Spirit.

From a spiritual perspective, we are children and women of the Almighty God. We are His workmanship; created in His likeness and image. We were created to worship Him and be witnesses of Him to others. Our commission is to spread the gospel of Christ.

We must learn how to balance the natural and spiritual areas of our life. We can be who we were designed to be. We can be compassionate and caring, yet allow God's Spirit to guide and lead us so our compassion and emotions do not choose for us. How many times have you been in a relationship and once it was over ask yourself, "What was I thinking?!"

At this season of your life you may need to reexamine your standards. That does not mean lower them but rather examine them to determine if they are realistic. Some of our standards were developed in our younger years and we have never taken a closer look at them as we have matured.

One thing I do want to make clear is that sometimes you can set standards so high that you may eliminate yourself from the equation and you do not want that. It may be a good idea to talk with godly counsel to discuss your expectations regarding relationships so they can give you realistic feedback. There is nothing wrong with high standards but you have to make sure they are attainable.

"How many times have you been in a relationship and once it was over asked yourself, What Was I Thinking?"

7
"MR. RIGHT" OR "MR. WHAT WAS I THINKING?"

The bible tells us, "You will know a tree by the fruit it bears." (Matthew 7:16). Therefore, when a man approaches you, see what fruit he is bearing before making a move.

Fruit Inspector

As a consumer, when you go to the market to buy fruit you usually inspect it first. You pick it up, examine it, and squeeze to make sure you are getting a quality product. Have you ever bitten into an apple that looked sweet only to find out that it was rotten on the inside? What's even worse, it had a worm? Yuck! Well, dating is similar to this process. The only good thing about bad fruit is that you have the option to return it to the store for an exchange. Therefore in relationships, you must inspect and investigate your potential husband's fruit.

Keep in mind that people generally look their best when dating. You only see the outer appearance, which can be a huge deception. What truly matters is what is in the heart of a man and his relationship with God. Therefore we should use all of our senses when dating including spiritual discernment which is the most important of them all.

The Counterfeit

Do not fall for the counterfeit! In other words, do not be taken in by someone who appears to be genuine but in reality they are a phony. The man approaching you may not be sent by God. Remember, the enemy knows your likes and dislikes; he will not send you an ungodly, uneducated man if you are believing God for a godly, educated man. Nor will the enemy send you someone who is sloppy, immature and foolish when you are believing for someone who is impeccable, mature and intelligent.

The enemy knows exactly what type of man you want. Therefore, you must take time in the relationship to find out all you can about the man you are dating. Allow time for your spirit to discern. If you fail to do so, your emotions may allow you to ignore all the RED, YELLOW and BLUE flags that present themselves in the early stages of the relationship. Once you become emotionally or sexually involved, you tend to overlook the blinding signs of a counterfeit.

In today's society, you really have to be serious when dating. After all, this is your life we are talking about here! Are you currently dating or considering dating someone who may be a phony? What are the characteristics of a counterfeit? You can define a counterfeit as someone or something that is not genuine.

Check the characteristics list to see if the man you are dating is possibly a counterfeit:

Counterfeit	Genuine
Irresponsible	Responsible
Unfaithful	Faithful
Lacks integrity	Has integrity
Not true to his word	Reliable
Selfish	Thoughtful
Prideful/Arrogant	Humble
Lacks goals	Goal oriented
Rude	Respectful
Inconsiderate	Considerate
Inconsistent	Consistent

Keep in mind that the man you are dating could have characteristics from both columns. Ultimately the deciding factor is what you consider a deal breaker.

Another exercise is to create a list of Pro's and Con's listing each item in the order of importance. Include the characteristics listed above. What does this say about the man you are dating?

Ask God and others about this person. Others may see something in him that is in your blind spot. Only ask people that you fully trust and have your best interest at heart. This can also be someone that does not have an emotional relationship with you because they can give an unbiased opinion. Ultimately you will make your own decisions, but input from others can help you make the best decision. The best decisions may hurt now but you will thank God later!

> **"You will know a tree by the fruit it bears."**
> **(Matthew 7:16)**

8
Mr. RIGHT QUESTIONNAIRE

Are you currently dating? Do you think he is *the one*? It is time to figure it out. Get your paper and pen and answer the following questions:

1. Is he saved?

2. What does his fruit say about him?

3. What kind of relationship does he have with his mother? (Generally this may indicate how he treats you.)

4. If you ask others who know him, what would they say about his character and integrity?

5. What are his interest (educational, career and hobbies) and are you compatible?

6. How does he treat you? Like a queen or does he expect you to treat him like a king instead. In other words, is his priority himself?

7. Do you feel like he found a treasure in you, or is he your treasure? (This will indicate if you value yourself).

8. How does he treat you around his friends, family and co-workers? Is it different when you're alone?

9. How is his behavior around other women? Is he respectful at all times or does he have roaming eyes and questionable behavior? (A gentleman is a gentleman no matter his surroundings.)

10. How does he respond when women are drawn to him? Is he flirtatious?

11. Does he show signs of jealousy or control?

12. Why did his previous relationship fail?
(It is very important to get to the root of this question. Generally if a man left his wife to be with you there is a great chance he will leave you for the next relationship. He is not loyal.)

13. Is he gainfully employed or self employed?

14. How are his finances: savings, retirement, and insurances?

15. Can he take care of you and a family?

16. Does he have an emergency fund?

17. What is his kingdom assignment? Does it correlate with your kingdom assignment? Both of you can be saved and have an assignment but are you compatible?

18. How does your assignment compliment his?

19. What are his feelings about marriage? What does marriage look like to him, i.e., his expectations?

20. Is he willing to do whatever it takes to please you and to cover you?

21. Has he had any trouble with the law? If so, what is the status; past and present.

22. Does he own a house?

23. Do you know his health status?

24. Have you introduced him to your friends and family? If not, why?

25. Are you considering pre-marital counseling? (It needs to be Godly and address intimate relationship details.)

26. Have you had a heart-to-heart with God about him?

27. Was he previously married?

28. Does he have children and how do they feel about you? How do you feel about them?

God has called the man to cover, protect and provide not only materially for a woman but emotionally and spiritually as well. You should be richer in mind, body and spirit. The man in your life should make rich deposits into your heart and spirit, not withdrawals. You should be treated like the queen that you are.

Remember, let God choose and send you your mate! Until He does, enjoy being single and use that time to work on YOU.

> **"Never allow someone to be your priority while allowing yourself to be their option."**
> Samuel Langhorne Clemens (Mark Twain)

9
PREPARING FOR YOUR MATE QUESTIONNAIRE

You must have faith and believe that it is God's will for you to be married. While you are waiting, start preparing for the manifestation of your mate.

Get your pen and paper again.

_____ (your name), if you found out today that the man you have been dating is your future husband, would you really be ready? Or will you have to delay the wedding because you have not considered what a long-term commitment truly means?

DATING

1. What do you have in common?

2. Do your lives complement each other?

3. Do you enjoy doing things together?

4. Are you attending the same church together? It helps you to know you are both receiving the same teaching.

5. Do you value each other's feelings and opinions?

COURTSHIP AND PREPARING FOR MARRIAGE

If you had 6-12 months to prepare for your wedding and become a married woman, the answers to the following questions may tell you if you are ready for marriage.

Finances

1. How are your finances?

2. Are you entering your marriage with a lot of debt?

3. If you have debt, what plan of action do you have to eliminate it?

4. Have you discussed your debt with your future husband?

Housing

5. Have you discussed living arrangements?

6. Do either of you own a house? If so, which house will you reside in?

7. Is there a realistic plan in place to sell or rent the other house?

Children

8. Do either of you want or have children?

9. Have you discussed, in great detail, the responsibility or role each will play in raising the children?

10. Have you created a relationship with his family and/or children?

11. Are either of you coming from a previous marriage? If so, how do you feel about that? Has he revealed to you why the marriage ended?

12. What do you have to offer this man of God?

These are the types of questions you need to answer before entering marriage.

Intensely look at your relationship and discern if he is the one. Remember, the wedding has not happened yet so you still have time to change your mind or delay the process. It is better to speak up early than to wait until the last minute. **If you know in your spirit that something is wrong, put on the brakes.**

10
DEFINING A VIRTUOUS WOMAN

Are you a Proverbs 31 woman? Not that you are totally comparing yourself to her but she is the pentacle. Do you have any of her characteristics? Please see the following characteristics of a Proverbs 31 woman. Do you see yourself?

Elaborate on how these scriptures bear witness to you. For example, Proverbs 12:4 says, "A virtuous woman is a crown to her husband." How will you be a crown to your husband? You can indicate, "I will be a crown to my husband by letting him be the leader of the home and praying for him."

PROVERBS 31:10-31

[10] Who can find a virtuous wife? For her worth is far above rubies.

¹¹The heart of her husband safely trusts her; so he will have no lack of gain.

¹²She does him good and not evil all the days of her life.

¹³She seeks wool and flax, and willingly works with her hands.

¹⁴She is like the merchant ships, she brings her food from afar.

¹⁵She also rises while it is yet night, and provides food for her household, and a portion for her maidservants.

¹⁶She considers a field and buys it; from her profits she plants a vineyard.

¹⁷She girds herself with strength, and strengthens her arms.

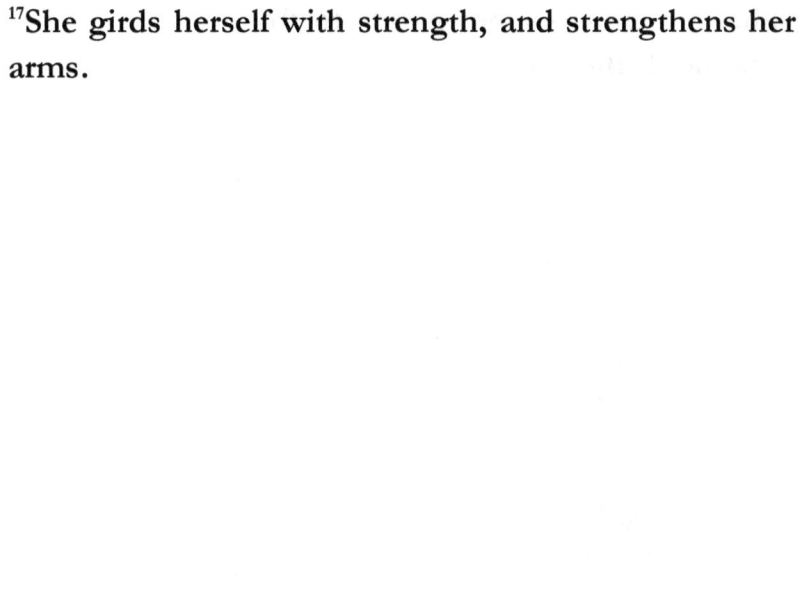

¹⁸She perceives that her merchandise is good, and her lamp does not go out by night.

[19]She stretches out her hands to the distaff, and her hand holds the spindle.

[20]She extends her hand to the poor, yes, she reaches out her hands to the needy.

[21]She is not afraid of snow for her household, for her all her household is clothed in scarlet.

[22]She makes a tapestry for herself; her clothing is fine linen and purple.

²³Her husband is known in the gates, when he sits among the elders of the land.

²⁴She makes linen garments and sells them, and supplies sashes for the merchants.

[25]Strength and honor are her clothing; she shall rejoice in time to come.

[26]She opens her mouth with wisdom, and on her tongue is the law of kindness.

²⁷She watches over the ways of her household, and does not eat the bread of idleness.

²⁸Her children rise up and call her blessed; her husband also, and he praises her:

[29]Many daughters have done well, but you excel them all.

[30]Charm is deceitful and beauty is passing, but a woman who fears the Lord, she shall be praised.

[31]Give her the fruit of her hands, and let her own works praise her in the gates.

11
A LETTER TO OUR DAUGHTERS

Dear Daughter,

Please understand that you are a rare find – a jewel! Do not let anyone treat you like a cheap imitation.

You want to be cautious when it comes to making promises or commitments. Making a commitment to God to live for him is the most important commitment you can make. Making a commitment to honor your parents is another important commitment. Committing to honor yourself and your body are commitments that are <u>very</u> important and need your attention.

Honor yourself by valuing your beliefs, opinions, and ideas instead of agreeing with what everyone else says. It means doing what you know to be right and best for you, while everyone else is doing something different.

Making a commitment to honor your body means to dress yourself in a way that tells others you are beautiful and require respect. It means eating in a way that will keep you healthy. Honoring your body means giving only one person, your husband, the privilege of sharing it.

You don't want to give your body away as if it has no value. The bible tells us that we are a royal priesthood. You want to strive to maintain your purity. The following scripture says it best: "Do not cast your pearls before swine" (Matthew 7:6). In other words, don't give your love, body or affection to someone or something undeserving.

If you are already in a relationship, decide if you need to make any changes. If you need help with this, connect with someone that understands where you are and can help you develop a prayer life. Prayer will help you think about the things God wants for your life.

It is never too late to make changes if you have made mistakes. When it comes to sex, please know that you have the right and the privilege to decide to abstain at any time. You should begin by asking yourself questions such as, "Why am I having sex?" or "Is this the person that I want for a husband?" It is not too late.

As a young lady there are so many things you can focus on right now that will lead to wonderful outcomes. Find things to do with your time such as meeting with friends, discussing career goals and dreams, or just having fun. Know that God is for you and He sees you as being lovely.

AUTHOR'S FINAL THOUGHTS

God wants good things for you. He wants you to be whole and have joy in Him. Then He wants the opportunity to show you, his daughter, how much he loves you by presenting a man that will love you like He does.

And while you wait remember...

"...*She* who waits on the Lord shall renew *her* strength; *she* shall mount up with wings like eagles, *she* shall run and not be weary, *she* shall walk and not faint." (Isaiah 40:31)

www.ingramcontent.com/pod-product-compliance
Lightning Source LLC
Chambersburg PA
CBHW060425050426
42449CB00009B/2142